准备过冬

Sharing the Planet | Non-Fiction Series

Copyright © 2022 by Level Learning, INC. and Washington Yu Ying PCS™
Original and Edited Text Copyright © 2022 by Washington Yu Ying PCS™

All rights reserved. No part of this book in whole or part may be reproduced without written permission from the publisher.

Published by Level Learning, INC.

Content Contributors:
Washington Yu Ying PCS™ - Qianyi (Shirley) Zhang, Pearl Zao He You
Level Learning - Jingyao Qi

Illustrations by: Josh Taira

Leveling classification based on Level Learning standard.
For full description, visit www.levellearning.com

ISBN 978-1-64040-053-5
Simplified Chinese Edition

About Level Learning:
Level Learning provides a literacy focused curriculum specifically designed for K-12 Chinese as a Second Language classrooms. Our program offers 20 levels of specific and detailed objectives, leveled texts and passages, mastery-based online assessment, and analytics to enable data-driven instruction. Level Learning reading curriculum for both literature and informational text emphasize grammar and comprehension skills to help teachers develop confident and independent Chinese language readers. The non-fiction series of books are specifically designed to support our informational text course based on multiple national standards. To learn more about our entire offering, visit www.levellearning.com.

About Washington Yu Ying PCS™:
Washington Yu Ying PCS is a Mandarin English dual language immersion International Baccalaureate (IB) World school. Yu Ying's mission is to inspire and prepare young people to create a better world by challenging them to reach their full potential in a nurturing Chinese/English educational environment. Yu Ying's comprehensive IB, dual immersion curriculum equips students with global competencies for success in the real world. As a leader in immersion education, Yu Ying is determined to advance Chinese language programs and global citizenry education by helping other schools create and strengthen their Chinese programs. For more information, email: products@washingtonyuying.org

冬天就要到了。

在树下,一只松鼠在跑来跑去。

这只松鼠在做什么呢?

松鼠在找吃的东西。

它准备过冬了。

在河边，小青蛙都不见了。

青蛙去哪里了呢？

青蛙要在家里睡一整个冬天。

青蛙要准备过冬了。

看天上，一群大雁飞过天空。

这群大雁要去哪里呢？

大雁要飞到温暖的地方。

大雁要准备过冬了。

冬天来了,你准备好过冬了吗?

Glossary

	Pinyin	English Definition
松鼠	sōng shǔ	squirrel
找	zhǎo	to search
准备	zhǔn bèi	to prepare
过冬	guò dōng	to get through winter
河边	hé biān	river bank
青蛙	qīng wā	frog
睡	shuì	sleep
整个	zhěng gè	entire
大雁	dà yàn	wild geese
天空	tiān kōng	sky
群	qún	flock
温暖	wēn nuǎn	warm

冬天来了,你准备好过冬了吗?

Glossary

	Pinyin	English Definition
松鼠	sōng shǔ	squirrel
找	zhǎo	to search
准备	zhǔn bèi	to prepare
过冬	guò dōng	to get through winter
河边	hé biān	river bank
青蛙	qīng wā	frog
睡	shuì	sleep
整个	zhěng gè	entire
大雁	dà yàn	wild geese
天空	tiān kōng	sky
群	qún	flock
温暖	wēn nuǎn	warm

www.ingramcontent.com/pod-product-compliance
Lightning Source LLC
Chambersburg PA
CBHW041224070526
44584CB00001B/83